THE VOICE OF
SHOOT

ANNUAL EDITOR: Kevin Pettman

 /TheVoiceOfFootball   WWW.SHOOT.CO.UK   @_shootfootball

CONTENTS

06	YOUR PROFILE
07	CLUB CREATOR
08	FACTS, STATS & NUMBERS
10	SHOOT CUP RUN
12	MYSTERY MANAGER
13	TRUE OR FALSE?
14	INTERVIEW: OLLIE WATKINS
16	SCRAMBLED STRIKERS
17	PROFILE: HOJBJERG
18	10 TOP 10s
20	MEGASTAR MATCH-UP
22	WORLD CUP WORDSEARCH
24	TALKING TACTICS
26	SUPER QUIZ – 1st HALF
28	INTERVIEW: ADAM WEBSTER
30	KIT SWITCH
31	PROFILE: FODEN
32	WSL SUPERHEROES
34	GOAL GREATS...
35	...ASSIST RATES
36	EYE KNOW YOU!
38	NORTH V SOUTH
40	DID YOU KNOW?
42	WHICH SEASON WAS IT?
44	2022 WINNERS
46	HIT OR MISS?
47	PROFILE: JAMES
48	INTERVIEW: ELLEN WHITE
50	SPOT THE BALL
52	SOCIAL SCENE
54	EUROPE'S TOP TEENS!
56	30 CHAMPIONS LEAGUE FACTS
58	PITCH PERFECT?
59	PROFILE: RAMSDALE
60	KLOPP'S CODE CRACKERS
62	GAMING STARS
64	SUPER QUIZ – 2nd HALF
66	INTERVIEW: CAROLINE WEIR
68	TRANSFER CHALLENGE
69	PROFILE: FERNANDES
70	YOUR WORLD CUP RECORDS
72	2023 WOMEN'S WORLD CUP
74	2023 THE FOOTY FUTURE
76	ANSWERS

THIS ANNUAL BELONGS TO /////////

NAME Harry pugh

AGE 10

FAVOURITE CLUB TEAM
Tottinhum hotspur

FAVOURITE NATIONAL TEAM
se rogot in k england

MY 5 FAVOURITE PLAYERS
1. sadia mug
2. niko o mitana
3. reece tames
4. son
5. kane

FAVOURITE MANAGER
core

TEAM I PLAY FOR
hhifhell a FC

MY POSITION
strong cf

CLUB CREATOR >>

Create a hot new dream team for 2023!

NEW CLUB NAME

FRANSIS WORRIOS *(handwritten)*

STAR PLAYER

Rorolomessi *(handwritten)*

DESIGN A CLUB KIT

TEAM FC WARRIOS *(handwritten in badge)*

STADIUM NAME

The Kings warros *(handwritten)*

LEAGUE PLAYING IN

Leetue of Geford *(handwritten)*

DESIGN A CLUB BADGE

WEMBLEY WOE

This year Mason Mount saw more Wembley misery. He lost the FA Cup and League Cup final, adding to two other cup final losses there with Chelsea, the Euro 2020 final with England and the play-off final with Derby!

AWAY KANE

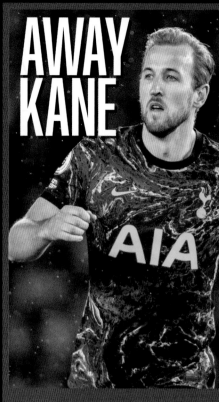

With a goal at Brighton this year, Harry Kane set a record for most Premier League strikes away from home. It was his 95th in just 139 away appearances and it beat Wayne Rooney's mark of 94!

FACTS, STATS & NUMBERS

Check out these memorable footy facts, stats and numbers from the biggest players and competitions this year!

KLOPP CLAIM

Liverpool's Jurgen Klopp became just the second manager to win the Champions League, FA Cup, League Cup and Premier League while with the same English club. The first was former Manchester United boss Sir Alex Ferguson.

RELEGATION RECORD

Norwich were relegated from the Premier League for a record sixth time. The Canaries have been sent straight back down in each of their last four top-flight seasons — 2021-22, 2019-20, 2015-16 and 2013-14.

LETHAL LEWY

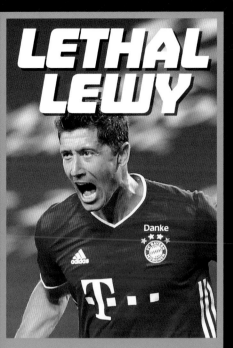

Bayern Munich legend Robert Lewandowski won the Bundesliga top scorer trophy for the seventh time (and fifth in a row) in 2022. That equals the achievement of Gerd Muller in the 1960s and '70s.

AWESOME ATTENDANCE

Barcelona's Champions League quarter-final with Real Madrid saw the biggest ever crowd for a women's match. Played at the Nou Camp, 91,553 fans watched Barca win 5-2 and it beat the previous best of 90,195 set by the USA in 1999.

HIGH FIVE

After winning the Spanish title with Real Madrid, Carlo Ancelotti is the first manager to have league success in Europe's top five leagues. He's also lifted the title in England (Chelsea), Germany (Bayern Munich), Italy (AC Milan) and France (PSG).

KING OF THE CHAMPIONSHIP

Fulham striker Aleksandar Mitrovic struck 43 goals for Fulham in the Championship, which is more than any other player in the competition's history!

ASSIST MACHINE

In 2022, Arsenal Women attacking star Beth Mead reached 36 assists in the Women's Super League. No other WSL ace has set up as many goals as mega Mead!

50TH HAT-TRICK

Cristiano Ronaldo bagged the 50th hat-trick of his club career. His three strikes for Manchester United against Norwich added to 49 others while playing for United, Real Madrid and Juventus.

SHOOT

CUP RUN

Play against a friend and tackle each cup round. If you get all the answers correct, move to the next round. Who'll reach the final and win? Ask a third person to read the answers so you don't accidentally see them. Good luck!

1st ROUND

CAPTAIN'S ARM BANDS

Name these three captains to move to the next round!

A **B** **C**

2nd ROUND

SPOT THE BEARD

A **B** **C**

The next round awaits if you can guess who these beards belong to!

3rd ROUND

WHAT'S MY NUMBER?

A SAKA

B MOUNT

C ALEXANDER-ARNOLD

Choose from these numbers to complete each player's missing number. Remember, a place in the quarter finals is up for grabs!

19 **10** **5**

66 **7** **29**

QUARTER FINAL
BADGE MASH

To reach the semis, work out which two Premier League club badges make up each one of these badge mash-ups!

 **A**

 **B** YOU'LL NEVER WALK ALONE · EST·1892

 **C** LONDON

CONOR COADY
CHRISTIAN PULISIC
HUGO LLORIS

FRANCE

ENGLAND

USA

SEMI FINAL
COUNTRY CONNECTION

Match the correct nation to each of these stars. The final is so close you can smell it!

THE FINAL
MASCOT MATCH-UP

You've made it all the way to the cup final! But a cup final is not complete without a club mascot to entertain the fans. Can you guess which clubs these mascots belong to? Let's see who will be going home with the silverware!

 **A**

 **B**

 **C**

PENALTY SHOOT-OUT

If there is no winner after the final question, the cup winners will be decided by this penalty shoot-out question. The player who gets closest to the correct answer will lift the cup! Are you ready? Here we go...

Q: What is the timing of the fastest goal in a Champions League final?

ANSWERS ON PAGES 76-77

MYSTERY MANAGER

Can you guess who these managers are from the clever clues and the shadowy picture?

MANAGER 1

Clue 1: Won a title with The Gers.

Clue 2: Always 'red-y' for action as a player.

Clue 3: Became a Premier League boss in 2021.

MANAGER 2

Clue 1: Won the FA Cup in first managerial season.

Clue 2: Was always Gunner become a top coach.

Clue 3: Played for a London club for five years.

MANAGER 3

Clue 1: Played in Spain and Italy.

Clue 2: First won the Champions League as boss in 2009.

Clue 3: Good mates with Messi.

MANAGER 4

Clue 1: First manager's job at Middlesbrough.

Clue 2: Captained every club he played for.

Clue 3: Coaches stars like Kane, Sterling and Saka.

ANSWERS ON PAGES 76-77

TRUE ////// OR FALSE?

It's time to work out the footy fact from the footy fiction! Tick your answer to each.

1
Arsenal keeper Aaron Ramsdale has played in the Premier League as well as the Championship, League One and League Two.

T F

2
The Tottenham Hotspur Stadium is the Premier League ground with the largest capacity.

T F

3
Manchester City legend Sergio Aguero scored 12 league hat-tricks for the club.

T F

4
Leicester defender Jonny Evans has more than 50 yellow cards in the Premier League.

T F

5
Mason Mount has won the Premier League twice.

T F

6
Mo Salah and Sadio Mane have both scored over 100 Premier League goals.

T F

ANSWERS ON PAGES 76-77

13

OLLIE WATKINS

The Aston Villa and England striker chats to *SHOOT* about hitting the net and working hard for club and country.

This year you wore the iconic England number nine for the first time. What was that like?

"It was quite cool. When I walked into the dressing room at Wembley I didn't expect to see number nine! I had number 19 a few days before in the Switzerland game, so I thought I'd be 19 again. When I saw 'Watkins' and the number nine it was quite cool."

That was the Ivory Coast game when you scored your second goal on your first start, didn't you?

"Yeah, it was a massive moment for me and something I have always thought about. Since I got into the England setup, I've always wanted to start a game rather than come off the bench. To do that was a big achievement in itself, then to score as well topped it off."

Did scoring on your England debut in 2021 help you?

"I think so. Also, in some of the games I have come on in I feel like I have been literally an inch away from scoring as well, so I probably could have scored a couple more. I'm really enjoying when I get called up and the opportunity to play for my country and just trying to embrace it whenever I get that opportunity."

Who has helped you settle internationally?

"At club level there is Tyrone Mings and then Jack Grealish, who was at Aston Villa previously. That's kind of like a comfort blanket! I also get on well with Luke Shaw and Mason Mount. They are both good lads."

There's a World Cup this year – have you always enjoyed big tournaments?

"World Cups are huge and where the biggest teams are. I remember seeing Ronaldinho and Zidane and looking at all these players when I was younger. It's the biggest competition and the biggest trophy to win in the world. I always look forward to it."

It feels like it's an exciting time to be at Aston Villa?

"It's a really exciting club to be at and I'm really enjoying my time here. It's the best place to be at really and to grow as a player. There are a lot of exciting things to come from us as a club. I'm really enjoying it."

Did you feel pressure joining Villa from Brentford for a club record fee?

"There was a lot of pressure, it was a hefty price tag for a Championship player and was a record transfer fee. There's pressure for me to deliver and help the team and score goals. I just wanted to try and enjoy it, make my family proud and I knew that if put my head down and worked hard then good things will come."

AVFC

Is your 'perfect' hat-trick against Liverpool a career highlight?

"I hadn't scored in the league going into that game, so to get a hat-trick was not what I expected – or the 7-2 score! It definitely took pressure off myself and I started to play with a little bit more freedom. Each game I grew and grew and got better I think."

Do you look at your time in the EFL and appreciate where you are now?

"I think I appreciate where I have come from. I don't take each day for granted and keep working hard. Just coming from grass roots makes you realise how lucky you are when you step into Tottenham's new stadium, The Emirates or playing at Villa Park each week. It makes you appreciate it. I have really enjoyed the journey so far and there's a long way still to go."

Have you always liked being a striker and scoring and creating?

"I have played all over really, but I always find myself wanting to score goals and wanting to create chances. That's definitely where I see myself and where I really enjoy playing."

Are there players you have looked at to perhaps learn from?

"Cristiano Ronaldo is an icon. The way he looks after himself and he always performs when people doubt him. He's definitely someone I look up to."

FACT FILE

CLUB: Aston Villa
COUNTRY: England
POSITION: Forward
BORN: 30 December 1995
PREVIOUS CLUBS:
Brentford, Exeter City,
Weston-super-Mare (loan)

FOOTY FAVES...

FAVE PLAYER OF ALL TIME:
Thierry Henry and Cristiano Ronaldo
FAVE SHIRT NUMBER: *14*
FAVE GOAL SCORED:
For Exeter against Plymouth in the Devon derby
FAVE FOOTBALL MEMORY: *My England debut*
FAVE KIT AS A KID: *Arsenal kit with the O2 sponsor*

SCRAMBLED STRIKERS

The names of these goal grabbers have been mixed up. Your job is to write each one correctly under the picture.

MERIT OWNER

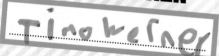

Tino werner

COD OR WISH

CB Wood

ACTION HALO MINI

Miche Cantona

JAYME RAVID

ACHED SAM

ANTI ENVOY

ANSWERS ON PAGES 76-77

HOJBJERG

NAME: Pierre-Emile Hojbjerg
CLUB: Tottenham
COUNTRY: Denmark
POSITION: Central midfield
BORN: 5 August 1995
PREVIOUS CLUBS: Southampton, Schalke, FC Augsburg, Bayern Munich

DID YOU KNOW?

Hojbjerg reached 50 Premier League games in a row for Tottenham last season – 'the Viking' hates missing a minute of the action!

17

TOP 10s

Let's run down ten of the best number 10s this year. What a brilliant bunch of attacking heroes!

1 NEYMAR

To have the iconic number 10 shirt at PSG and Brazil, you need to be something super special... and Neymar is! His goals and skills have delivered trophies and awards all over the world.

2 KYLIAN MBAPPE

World Cup hero Mbappe proudly wears 10 for France, following in the footsteps of guys like Zidane and Platini. He scores, creates and pulls defenders all over the pitch with his fierce forward powers.

3 LUKA MODRIC

To own the eye-catching number 10 at Real Madrid, and as the captain of Croatia, for so long shows how influential little Luka has been in the game! He's 37 now but still bosses it.

4 HARRY KANE

Spurs legend Kane wasn't quite as prolific for Tottenham in 2021-22, but the England captain was still involved with 26 Premier League goals in total. Kane can lead the attacking line or drop back as a classic number 10!

5
CHRISTIAN PULISIC

Pulisic took the 10 shirt ahead of the 2020-21 season and his Chelsea stats are impressive. In his first 67 league games he was involved in 24 goals and has plenty of trophies to show off!

6
GEORGIA STANWAY

At Manchester City Stanway became the club's record women's scorer in 2022, blasting 64 in just 170 games! She was a classy number 10 at City before leaving for Bayern Munich in the summer!

JENNI HERMOSO

Awesome Hermoso has five league titles with Barcelona Women, as well as the Champions League and a stack of cups. It's no surprise she's the top scorer for Barca and Spain – a perfect 10!

7

8
ANSU FATI

Can you imagine taking over the 10 shirt from Messi at Barcelona? That's what Fati did! The youngster has much to follow but, luckily, he's got it all in his locker to become another top 10.

9
JACK GREALISH

Some 10s in this rundown are complete goal machines with natural striking abilities. At Manchester City, Grealish plays more behind the striker or drifts in from wide for maximum attacking threat!

10

LIONEL MESSI

Any list of magical number 10s has to include the wizardry of Lionel Messi! He still wears the famous shirt for Argentina and reached 750 career goals last season. Proper legend!

MEGASTAR MATCH-UP

Which awesome player are you most like?
Tick the four footy phrases that best describe you to find out!

It's a total shock if you don't hit the net every week!

A hard working team player who enjoys playing behind a main striker.

From free-kicks and set pieces you're the best in the business!

Since joining your team you have stacked up lots of games for your club.

You're desperate to win club trophies for the first time.

You regularly smash league and club records.

It's important to keep a happy face on the pitch.

When you join a club, you give it your all and want to be a legend.

Energy, enthusiasm and smart tactical sense are what power your game.

MOSTLY

You and **Robert Lewandowski** are so similar! The Poland ace is a goal machine and as you both have net-busting skills your club is guaranteed success.

You love central midfield but can also do a decent job in defence.

MOSTLY

Every team needs a powerhouse hero like you and **Declan Rice**! The enforcer is loved by the fans and adoration like that lifts your performances to even higher levels.

Seven is the best shirt number to have!

MOSTLY

You're a great match with **Son Heung-min**. The Tottenham and South Korea forward delivers with goals, assists, top team play and a happy face – just like you!

Being a leader on the pitch comes naturally to you.

MOSTLY

James Ward-Prowse and you could be related! As slick, reliable and creative midfielders you're both one of the first names on the manager's team sheet.

WORLD CUP
WORDSEARCH

Can you spot all 20 of these international stars hiding in the grid?

VAN DIJK

KANE

GRIEZMANN

CASEMIRO

MESSI

MAGUIRE

DEPAY

KANTE

BALE

GNABRY

ALISSON

NEYMAR

MITROVIC

DE BRUYNE

MORATA

HOJBJERG

STERLING

RUDIGER

MODRIC

LUKAKU

22

K	O	L	A	T	X	L	S	M	R	P	R	D	U	M	A	F	N
E	C	I	Z	L	U	V	H	B	X	U	B	L	V	Q	I	D	R
W	C	G	M	K	I	F	F	T	R	H	D	S	J	P	V	O	Q
V	W	X	A	W	T	S	L	W	U	A	W	I	C	Q	A	V	N
J	F	K	L	Z	H	Z	S	A	E	T	J	Y	G	P	B	M	M
K	U	G	N	A	B	R	Y	O	U	A	W	J	A	E	E	C	N
I	E	V	Z	J	G	K	H	L	N	R	O	Z	C	P	R	G	E
T	G	T	K	L	A	P	B	P	R	O	Z	T	X	F	E	Z	Y
P	Q	R	C	I	V	O	R	T	I	M	X	M	I	O	W	D	M
W	J	B	I	O	J	T	C	S	T	E	R	L	I	N	G	T	A
X	L	Y	B	E	V	E	K	D	V	E	G	C	X	H	Q	L	R
N	O	N	X	L	Z	K	B	A	T	T	V	D	O	K	X	V	S
O	D	N	I	Y	W	M	N	P	G	N	V	U	P	G	G	T	O
P	O	L	C	A	Y	D	A	R	C	A	S	L	L	R	C	I	R
E	R	O	O	S	I	B	E	N	O	K	J	C	F	P	A	F	A
O	N	C	L	J	L	J	C	X	N	F	C	E	M	V	N	Q	I
R	J	Y	K	A	B	M	K	F	J	Z	A	E	N	Z	M	M	F
U	S	H	U	J	Z	Y	Z	O	M	P	S	Y	J	K	H	O	D
Q	C	S	O	R	K	S	P	L	I	S	E	D	C	U	L	D	C
E	S	H	D	O	B	A	A	D	I	K	M	Y	Q	A	E	R	O
E	B	G	F	B	B	E	X	V	E	B	I	V	M	L	F	I	N
O	I	O	P	Z	K	I	D	P	U	H	R	A	A	W	L	C	F
W	H	D	H	V	F	G	K	A	N	E	O	B	W	A	D	L	I
B	T	P	C	E	Y	C	Q	E	A	E	R	I	U	G	A	M	W

GOAL FEST

Harry Kane (England) and Memphis Depay (Netherlands) were Europe's highest scorers in World Cup qualifying. They each bagged 12 goals in their group.

WORLD CUP FIRST

Apart from Qatar, who earned a place as hosts, Germany were the first country to qualify for the 2022 World Cup. They sealed their spot in October 2021.

CHRISTMAS KICK-OFF

For the first time in its history, the World Cup will not take place in either June or July. Kicking off on the 21st November with the final just a week before Christmas day!

ANSWERS ON PAGES 76-77

"TALKING TACTICS"

To be a mega football fan you should know what the phrases, words, sayings and systems spoken about actually mean in a tactical team talk. Shoot has done the homework for you, so get reading and understanding!

TRANSITION

WHAT IT MEANS... Transition is the time straight after a team wins or loses possession of the ball. It's usually just a few seconds and the best players and teams know exactly what to do during transitions to create and score goals!

COMBINATIONS

WHAT IT MEANS... Quick passes made between a number of players on a team. Combinations can be great in tight spaces to allow a team to launch a speedy attack or to get the ball away from danger.

FALSE NINE

WHAT IT MEANS... A clever tactic where a player starts in a central striker position but then drops from being the furthest forward attacker to bring the other team's defenders out of position. Can be deployed by smaller, creative players.

PLAYING AS A TEN

WHAT IT MEANS... A player doesn't have to be wearing the number ten shirt to play as a number ten! This tactical role sees a skilful attacker link midfield with the forwards, often with a freedom to play in different positions.

OVERLAP

WHAT IT MEANS... Watch out for a right-back or left-back, or a wing back, running out wide and beyond a winger to make space further forward. Fast and attack-minded defenders are good at this.

LOW BLOCK

WHAT IT MEANS... If a team uses a low block tactic it means their defensive unit, of perhaps two centre-backs and two full-backs, will position their defensive line close to their own goal. The defence and midfield will play close to each other.

COUNTER ATTACK

WHAT IT MEANS... When a team wins the ball back, they will then go on the attack and move the ball forward quickly. This can catch the other team out, especially when players are not in the best position to defend the counter attack.

HIGH PRESS

WHAT IT MEANS... Now very common in professional football, a high press means a team runs and works hard to put pressure on the opposition to gain control of the ball near to the opponent's goal. Forwards and midfielders will 'press' and hassle players into making a mistake.

SWEEPER KEEPER

WHAT IT MEANS... A tactic that sees the goalkeeper regularly come out of their area to influence the play. In a way the goalkeeper acts like an extra defender to stop attacks and plays passes forward. A sweeper keeper needs good footwork.

COUNTER-PRESS

WHAT IT MEANS... If a coach demands that the players work to get the ball back quickly after losing it, this is called a counter-press. Counter-pressing is most effective in the final third of the pitch (the area in and around the other team's goal).

DID YOU KNOW?

Liverpool's brilliant boss Jurgen Klopp was named The Best FIFA Men's Coach in 2021 and 2020.

SHOOT'S SUPER QUIZ

FIRST HALF

Take SHOOT's tough test to work out the power of your footy brain! It's going to be a challenge and make sure you complete the second half on pages 64-65.

1

Which club did Christian Eriksen join in January 2022?

brentford

2

Who is this Manchester City and Portugal star?

ruben dias

3

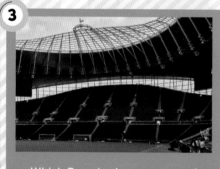

Which Premier League ground is this?

White hart lane

4

Marc-Andre ter Stegen plays for which country?

germany

5

Name this Manchester United manager in 2021-22.

Ralph rarnick

6

Which EFL club plays at Pride Park?

7

Who is this legendary French manager and former player?

zidane

8

Which position do Reece-James and Wan-Bissaka play?

cb

9

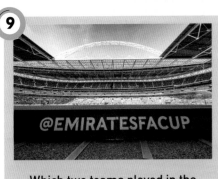

Which two teams played in the 2022 men's FA Cup final?

....

10

Name the club that plays home games at Craven Cottage.

....

11

What nationality is England women's manager Sarina Wiegman?

....

12

True or false? Mikel Arteta used to manage Spain.

....

13

What does VAR stand for?

....

14

In 2022, how many league titles had Bayern Munich won in a row?

....

15

Boavista, Braga and Maritimo are teams in which country?

....

16

Which football club are nicknamed The Hammers?

....

17

Can you name this hotshot Chelsea Women striker?

....

18

Pierre-Emerick Aubameyang switched Arsenal for which Spanish team in January 2022?

....

19

True or false? Rangers have won more league titles than Celtic.

....

20

Which number does James Maddison wear for Leicester City?

....

ANSWERS ON PAGES 76-77

ADAM WEBSTER

The Brighton defender talks to *SHOOT* about leading from the back, grabbing a few goals and his England dream.

This is your fourth Premier League season with Brighton. Do you feel very established now?

"Definitely. I feel comfortable. The 2020-21 season was probably when I really felt at home in the Premier League. I feel like that has shown in my performances and now hopefully I can help some of the younger lads as well."

Do you think of yourself as an experienced player?

"Yeah, well, sort of! There are a few older lads than me but there's a little group of us that are like leaders in the changing room and I certainly see myself as one of them. Younger players than me, like Neal Maupay, have played a lot of games too. We have quite a bit of experience in the team now, which is good."

Are you a vocal player who enjoys leading?

"I'd say I'm quite vocal and I have grown into it. When I was at Ipswich I was young and had senior pros barking orders! At Bristol we had quite a young squad, so I had to bring that side of my game out more. The manager there, Lee Johnson, put a microphone on my GPS vest in pre-season and the first league game. He could then watch the game back with my communication and see how I was communicating. I'd say since then I've really become more of a leader."

You have competition with some quality centre-backs, don't you?

"Definitely. Joel Veltman has done really well in the position this year. Before I came, I knew how good the Duffy-Dunk partnership was from watching them on TV for years. I always knew how good they were, so to learn from them every day was a big part for me in improving when I first came to Brighton."

How much do you enjoy keeping a clean sheet?

"It's important. It's not just the defenders, it's the whole team. We defend as a team and in this league it's hard to get clean sheets. Every team probably has international players at the top end! It's the best league in the world and never easy to come away with a clean sheet. When you do you've got to enjoy it and build on it."

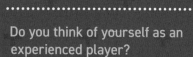

BRIGHTON & HOVE ALBION

FACT FILE

CLUB: Brighton
YEAR JOINED: 2019
COUNTRY: England
POSITION: Defender
BORN: 4 January 1995
PREVIOUS CLUBS: Bristol City, Ipswich, Aldershot (loan), Portsmouth

Brighton are very good tactically. Is that something you enjoy?

"It's really enjoyable. I'd say we're never predictable. Sometimes in games we'll change formation and adapt to that and new personnel. It's something we all have to do because every game is different in this league. You've got to be able to adapt and be versatile, otherwise it can become too predictable. I'd say we're definitely not predictable!"

You've also scored a few big goals for the club!

"I've scored against some of the big boys, which is nice! Clean sheets are obviously nice but when you score, there's nothing like it. You can't describe it sometimes and especially when it's an important goal. The adrenaline takes over and you can't really control yourself – well, I can't because I don't score that often!"

Would you like to make the England squad one day?

"Of course. I've always dreamed of playing for England. That's a huge goal of mine. Last season was frustrating because it was stop-start for me with injury and when I have played I've probably been playing the best I have in the Premier League. One day I'd like to say that I could play for England but right now I just need to focus on playing consistently and playing well."

FOOTY FAVES...

FAVE PLAYER OF ALL TIME: *Lionel Messi*

FAVE AWAY GROUND: Tottenham's new stadium is amazing

FAVE GOAL SCORED: Equaliser against Man. City in 2021

FAVE FOOTBALL MEMORY: Beckham's free-kick for England against Greece in 2001

FAVE FORMER TEAMMATE: Conor Chaplin, Ipswich

Credit: BHAFC/Paul Hazlewood

KIT SWITCH

These four footy fellas have had their kits mixed up. Get the correct shirt, shorts and socks back to each one!

A

B

C

D

A

B

C

D

A

B

C

D

RAUL JIMENEZ
SHIRT — C
SHORTS — B
SOCKS — D

TRENT ALEXANDER-ARNOLD
SHIRT — D
SHORTS — A
SOCKS — C

JAMES TAVERNIER
SHIRT — B
SHORTS — D
SOCKS — A

OLLIE WATKINS
SHIRT
SHORTS
SOCKS

ANSWERS ON PAGES 76-77

FODEN

NAME: Phil Foden
CLUB: Manchester City
COUNTRY: England
POSITION: Midfielder/forward
BORN: 28 May 2000
PREVIOUS CLUBS: None

DID YOU KNOW?

In 2018 Foden became the youngest player to earn a Premier League winners' medal. He was just 17 years and 350 days old!

WOMEN'S SUPER LEAGUE
SUPERHEROES

The Women's Super League (WSL) is packed with out-of-this-world stars! Power your way through this awesome guide to some of the greats!

SAM KERR

SUPER POWER

NET-BUSTING SHOOTING

Kerr has crashed in the goals since arriving at Chelsea in 2020. This year the Australian netted her 50th for the club in 69 appearances and also a record 50th for her country, Australia. Stopping Kerr from getting on the scoresheet takes all the top defenders in the WSL galaxy!

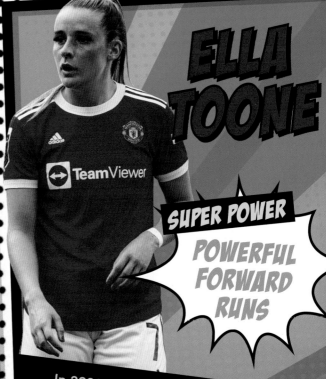

ELLA TOONE

SUPER POWER

POWERFUL FORWARD RUNS

In 2022, attacking threat Ella Toone became the first to play 100 games for Manchester United. In that century she struck 40 goals and as part of the team that won the Championship in 2019 she's already a club legend. Toone scored a hat-trick in just her sixth England appearance!

KATIE McCABE

SUPER POWER

DAZZLING WING PLAY

Every Women's Super League team would love to have a superstar like McCabe! The Arsenal ace can smash it as an awesome winger or drop back to a full-back role. Wherever magical McCabe pops up she can create, score, tackle and put in a match-winning performance.

ALESSIA RUSSO

SUPER POWER
SPEED & VISION

Watch out for the eye-catching forward making an even bigger name for herself in future WSL seasons. The fearsome forward has a natural scoring instinct for Manchester United and last season she also netted a hat-trick for England in just 11 minutes. Super impressive!

KHADIJA SHAW

SUPER POWER
STRENGTH & FINISHING

Already Jamaica's all-time top scorer, bagging 42 goals in her first 30 internationals, Shaw's super powers graced the WSL when she joined Manchester City last season. The tall forward is a menace for defenders and Shaw's link-up skills and work rate make her a constant threat!

ELLIE ROEBUCK

SUPER POWER
FLYING SAVES

The Manchester City and England goalkeeper pulls off amazing saves with her ability to speed through the air and her lightning-quick reflexes. Roebuck picked up the first-ever WSL Golden Glove award and she's already on the way to becoming an all-time hero for club and country!

FRAN KIRBY

SUPER POWER
MAGICAL ATTACKING SKILLS

Fantastic forward Kirby became Chelsea's record goalscorer in 2020 and the following year reached a century of strikes for the WSL heavyweights. Kirby and Sam Kerr make a great superhero double act at Chelsea – they should have capes and masks!

KIM LITTLE

SUPER POWER
DYNAMIC MIDFIELD DISPLAYS

This year, Arsenal boss Jonas Eidevall described club captain Kim Little as "phenomenal" and a "legend." With words like that, the former Scotland international just has to be in the WSL superhero squad! Little's goals, passing, tackling and leadership show she's a class act.

GOAL GREATS...

How many goals did these legends score in the Premier League? Write one of the goal numbers listed by each player.

SERGIO AGUERO
MANCHESTER CITY
GOALS:

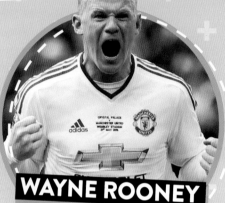

WAYNE ROONEY
MANCHESTER UNITED & EVERTON
GOALS:

PETER CROUCH
CLUBS INCLUDE: STOKE, TOTTENHAM, LIVERPOOL
GOALS:

THIERRY HENRY
ARSENAL
GOALS:

LUIS SUAREZ
LIVERPOOL
GOALS:

GOAL TOTALS

175
108
208
69
162
184
177

JERMAIN DEFOE
CLUBS INCLUDE: BOURNEMOUTH, SUNDERLAND, TOTTENHAM
GOALS:

FRANK LAMPARD
CHELSEA, MANCHESTER CITY, WEST HAM
GOALS:

34

ANSWERS ON PAGES 76-77

...ASSIST RATES!

Every goal legend needs an assist hero! See if you can guess the total Premier League assists each of these stars recorded from the list of options.

EDEN HAZARD
CHELSEA
ASSISTS:

DAVID SILVA
MANCHESTER CITY
ASSISTS:

OLIVIER GIROUD
ARSENAL & CHELSEA
ASSISTS:

JERMAINE JENAS
CLUBS INCLUDE: TOTTENHAM & NEWCASTLE
ASSISTS:

DAVID BECKHAM
MANCHESTER UNITED
ASSISTS:

ASSIST TOTALS

54
92
28
26
111
93
80

CESC FABREGAS
ARSENAL & CHELSEA
ASSISTS:

STEVEN GERRARD
LIVERPOOL
ASSISTS:

ANSWERS ON PAGES 76-77

EYE KNOW YOU!

Identify who these players are just from 'eyeing' them up! Use the clue if it helps.

1

CLUE Played for Liverpool, City, Villa and Newcastle.

....

2

CLUE Runs much quicker than he *walks*.

....

3

CLUE Rocked at Dortmund

....

4

CLUE Goalscoring defender.

....

5

CLUE Nicknamed Big Ben.

....

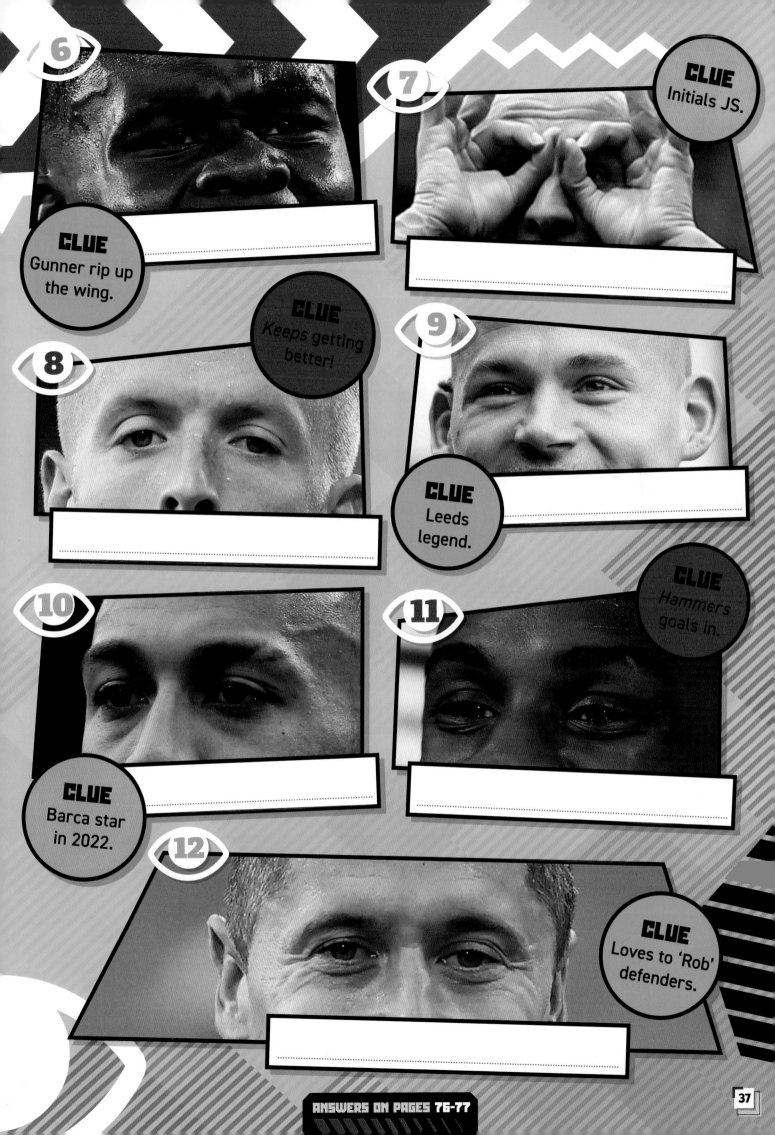

6

CLUE Gunner rip up the wing.

7

CLUE Initials JS.

CLUE Keeps getting better!

8

9

CLUE Leeds legend.

10

11

CLUE Hammers goals in.

CLUE Barca star in 2022.

12

CLUE Loves to 'Rob' defenders.

ANSWERS ON PAGES 76-77

NORTH

Ever wondered which region rules in English football – does the north or the south have more trophies? These stats and facts reveal the kings of the country!

Correct as of 1 June 2022.

PREMIER LEAGUE

NORTH: 21	SOUTH: 9

It's a huge win for the north in Premier League trophies. We've classed Leicester's amazing 2016 triumph as a victory for the south!

EUROPA LEAGUE

NORTH: 4	SOUTH: 5

The first Europa League final was 2010 and it was called the UEFA Cup before this. Adding both together gives the south a slim win – Ipswich Town were victorious here again in 1981!

CHAMPIONS LEAGUE

NORTH: 11	SOUTH: 3

Also including the old European Cup, the north takes a big win in European glory. Nottingham Forest's two titles (1979 and 1980) are for the north, with Aston Villa's in 1982 a triumph for the south!

FA CUP

NORTH: 72	SOUTH: 68

It's tight in the battle for most FA Cup final wins, and although Arsenal hold the record with 14 titles, it's the north who come out on top in this historic English competition.

v SOUTH

LEAGUE CUP

NORTH: 31 | **SOUTH: 30**

Just one win separates the north and south in the League Cup final! A southern club hasn't lifted the trophy since Chelsea in 2015.

FIFA CLUB WORLD CUP

NORTH: 2 | **SOUTH: 1**

Starting in 2000, three English clubs have won this world prize after victory in the Champions League final the season before. Manchester United, Liverpool and Chelsea are the lucky trio.

ALL ENGLAND CLUB

There were all-English, North v South, Champions League finals in 2008 (Manchester United v Chelsea), 2019 (Liverpool v Spurs) and 2021 (Chelsea v Manchester City).

UEFA SUPER CUP

NORTH: 6 | **SOUTH: 3**

Liverpool (4), Manchester United and Nottingham Forest score six UEFA Super Cup crowns for the north, with Chelsea's double and Aston Villa in 1982 claiming three for the south. Another northern success!

NORTHERN POWER

Although Arsenal were the first southern Premier League champions, in 1998, the first six titles all went to the north (Manchester United 5, Blackburn Rovers 1).

TOTAL — NORTH: 147 | SOUTH: 119

It's an easy win for the mighty northern clubs! The south has some serious catching up!

DID YOU

Rangers have won the most top-flight league titles by any club in the world. In 2021 the Scottish giants won their 55th championship, with their first coming back in 1891. Global greatness in Glasgow!

The success of Italian team **Juventus** far outweighs little **Notts County**, but they have a strong connection. Juve's famous black and white colours were actually taken from Notts County after the English club sent them their own footy shirts in 1903. Weird, huh?

Slick winger **Angel Di Maria** has seen huge transfers to Benfica, Real Madrid, Manchester United and PSG totalling over £150 million. One of his early moves as a kid in Argentina was for much less – he once transferred with his new club giving 35 footballs in return. Un-ball-ievable!

Italy goalkeeper **Gianluigi Donnarumma** likes wearing strange shirt numbers. At boyhood club AC Milan he had number 99 and after moving to PSG, where he wasn't allowed those digits, he instead picked 50. You should be showing off your no.1 status, pal!

KNOW?

Have you watched a game when zero corners were taken? Chelsea smashed Wigan 6-0 in 2010 and it's the only Premier League game not to see a single corner kick. Wigan were so bad that day they'd have celebrated like crazy if they had got one!

Striker **Fernando Torres** netted in an incredible seven competitions for Chelsea in 2012-13. These were the Premier League, Champions League, Europa League, FA Cup, League Cup, FIFA Club World Cup and Community Shield. If he'd bagged in the European Super Cup too it would have been a gr-eight result!

Cristiano Ronaldo is a goal king, but before him another Ronaldo was striking royalty. The original **Ronaldo** starred for the likes of Barcelona, Real Madrid and Brazil. Him and Cristiano only appeared together once while on opposite sides in a friendly in 2005. Double Ron-tastic!

Cristiano Ronaldo notched his 110th goal for Portugal in 2021 to make him the highest men's international goal scorer. He has a long, long, long way to go to beat Canada's **Christine Sinclair** though. In 2021 she netted her 188th international strike. See ya, C-Ron!

WHICH SEASON WAS IT?

There are hundreds of big moments every season and it's tricky to remember when stuff took place! In a test of your knowledge, pick the season when these things happened.

1

Chelsea lift the Champions League title.

Southampton promoted to the Premier League.

Roy Hodgson takes charge of England.

SEASON:

2

The Euro 2020 final goes to a penalty shootout.

Patrick Vieira becomes the Crystal Palace manager.

SEASON:

Raheem Sterling nets his 100th Premier League goal.

3

Leicester win the league title.

Harry Kane's first Premier League Golden Boot.

Portugal become Euro champions.

SEASON: 2016

4

Steven Gerrard plays his final game for Liverpool.

England Women finish third at the World Cup.

SEASON:

Hull, Burnley and QPR relegated from the Premier League.

PICK A SEASON FROM...

2004-05	2014-15	2015-16	2020-21	2017-18
1998-99	2011-12	2006-07	2021-22	2019-20

5

Wayne Rooney joins Everton.

Wolves win the Championship.

Real Madrid are European champions for 13th time.

SEASON:

6

Liverpool win the Champions League.

Chelsea win their first Premier League.

Lionel Messi opens his scoring account for Barcelona.

SEASON:

7

Arsenal begin playing at The Emirates.

Liverpool lose the Champions League final.

Walter Smith returns as Rangers manager.

SEASON:

8

Manchester United win the Treble.

Nottingham Forest relegated from the top flight.

Kevin Keegan manages England.

SEASON:

9

VAR is used in the Premier League.

Joao Cancelo transfers to Manchester City.

Liverpool are champions for first time since 1990.

SEASON:

10

Leah Williamson is the new England Women captain.

Fulham win the Championship.

Antonio Conte takes over as Tottenham boss.

SEASON:

FOOTBALL

ANSWERS ON PAGES 76-77

2022 WINNERS

This year has seen loads of awesome champions crowned. Take a look back at the winners from around the world, plus you can fill in the blanks. It's trophy time!

DOMESTIC

PREMIER LEAGUE
MANCHESTER CITY

FA CUP & LEAGUE CUP
LIVERPOOL

CHAMPIONSHIP
1ST: FULHAM

Promoted
Bournemouth,
Nottingham Forest (play-offs)

LEAGUE ONE
1ST: WIGAN

Promoted
Rotherham United,
Sunderland (play-offs)

LEAGUE TWO
1ST: FOREST GREEN ROVERS

Promoted
Exeter City, Bristol Rovers,
Port Vale (play-offs)

NATIONAL LEAGUE
1st: Stockport County
Promoted: Grimsby (play-offs)

SCOTTISH PREMIERSHIP
Celtic

SCOTTISH CUP
Rangers

SCOTTISH LEAGUE CUP
Celtic

NIFL PREMIERSHIP
Linfield

CYMRU PREMIER
The New Saints

COMMUNITY SHIELD

EUROPE

LA LIGA (Spain)
1st: Real Madrid
2nd: Barcelona

BUNDESLIGA (Germany)
1st: Bayern Munich
2nd: Borussia Dortmund

LIGUE 1 (France)
1st: Paris Saint-Germain
2nd: Marseille

SERIE A (Italy)
1st: Milan
2nd: Inter Milan

EREDIVISIE (Netherlands)
1st: Ajax
2nd: PSV Eindhoven

PRIMEIRA LIGA (Portugal)
1st: Porto
2nd: Sporting

CHAMPIONS LEAGUE

REAL MADRID

EUROPA LEAGUE

EINTRACHT FRANKFURT

EUROPA CONFERENCE

ROMA

WOMEN

WSL & FA CUP

CHELSEA

EUROPEAN SUPER CUP

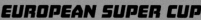
....

INTERNATIONAL

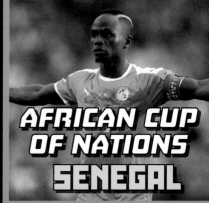

AFRICAN CUP OF NATIONS
SENEGAL

CHAMPIONS LEAGUE

LYON

LEAGUE CUP

MANCHESTER CITY

CHAMPIONSHIP
1st: Liverpool

MEN'S WORLD CUP

Argentina
....

WOMEN'S EUROS

....

NATIONS CUP (2023)

....

HIT OR MISS?

There's a glorious goalscoring chance in each of these pictures, but did the ball hit the back of the net or not? Take your guess!

GAME 1: Burnley V Liverpool

HIT or MISS? MISS

GAME 2: Brentford V Manchester City

HIT or MISS?  MISS

GAME 3: Atalanta V Manchester United

HIT or MISS? HIT

GAME 4: Brighton V Norwich

HIT or MISS? HIT

ANSWERS ON PAGES 76-77

JAMES

NAME: Reece James

CLUB: Chelsea

COUNTRY: England

POSITION: Right-back/wing-back

BORN: 8 December 1999

PREVIOUS CLUBS: Wigan (loan)

DID YOU KNOW?

His younger sister, Lauren, joined Chelsea Women in 2021 after playing for Manchester United and Arsenal.

ELLEN WHITE

SHOOT asks the awesome England striker about being a record goalscorer, her love for The Lionesses and her cool celebration!

What achievement would playing at a fourth World Cup in 2023 be?

"It has been a crazy couple of years for the world living in a pandemic. The Euros were pushed on a year, like the Olympics were, so we're coming off the back of a major tournament and a number of tournaments rolling in each summer. It is really exciting to be an England player and obviously there are some exciting things happening and the World Cup will be an incredible occasion."

Were you proud to become England women's record goalscorer last season?

"Yes of course. It was spoken about for a little while and I didn't really want to talk about it, because for me it was about playing for England, being selected and the team winning. I'm sure you can see with the emotion that I felt when it actually happened, being surrounded by my teammates and that celebration that it really meant a lot to me."

What did passing Kelly Smith's record feel like?

"I felt really emotional in the moment that I'd reached it and surpassed Kelly Smith, who was a big role model for me, a massive legend in the game and a big inspiration. So to surpass her record was amazing and something that I am really proud of and will look back on and be proud of."

You seem very passionate when you play for your country?

"I want to keep moving forward helping the team in any way I can – on and off the pitch – to do great things. I have a lot of pride being an England player and a lot of passion. I just love playing for England! I know ultimately my job is to score goals but if I can help the team achieve something really special then that is the big priority for me."

How would you sum up your role within the team?

"A forward that has lots of energy who loves to run around and help the team. My work rate will always be a given with me – I will work my absolute hardest for the team. Essentially my job is to score goals and be in the right position at the right time when the wingers have the ball or the midfield have the ball and be in the right place to score the goals."

There are lots of talented goalscorers in the squad! Beth Mead, Beth England and many more...

"It's a dream! I feel very lucky that I'm in a team where we've got phenomenal talent. You have named a few there but we've got Lauren Hemp, Alessia Russo, Ella Toone... we have got phenomenal individuals and I have got players at Manchester City that I get to train week in, week out with too. I am very lucky to be in a team where the talent is so good."

Finally, will your famous goal celebration continue?

"Of course! It will stay around! I do get a lot of questions and people talk about it and I get sent pictures of young girls and boys and adults doing that celebration. For me it's all about having fun, putting smiles on faces and showing how much you enjoy it and love football really, so that's why I love doing it."

FACT FILE

CLUB: **Manchester City**
COUNTRY: **England**
POSITION: **Forward**
BORN: **9 May 1989**
PREVIOUS CLUBS:
Birmingham City, Notts County, Arsenal, Leeds

SPOT THE BALL

Six balls have appeared in each of these footy photos.
Write down which is the real one for each.

GAME 1

ARSENAL V BRIGHTON

GAME 2

LEICESTER CITY V ASTON VILLA

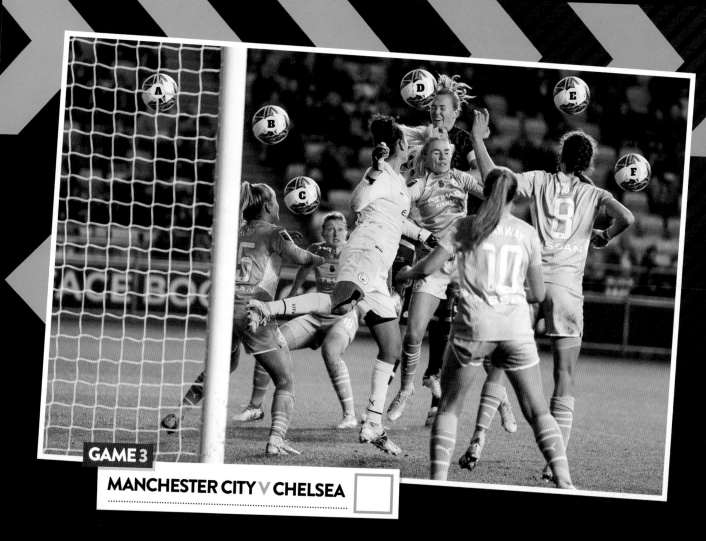

GAME 3

MANCHESTER CITY V CHELSEA

GAME 4

MANCHESTER UNITED V NORWICH CITY

ANSWERS ON PAGES 76-77

OFF THE PITCH...
SOCIAL SCENE

Want to see how the top players chill out away from the pitch? Check these pics from the biggest social media stars!

CRISTIANO RONALDO

CR7 is rocking it with his birthday cake. Tasty stuff!
Credit: @cristiano

Social Star

Ronaldo is the world's most followed footballer with over 440 million Instagram fans!

MASON MOUNT

Is it James Bond? Nah, but this smart style really 'suits' Mount!
Credit: @masonmount

LIONEL MESSI

Are Messi's skills out of this world? Well, here's the proof!
Credit: @leomessi

KYLIAN MBAPPE

Mbappe ditches the PSG kit for a slick look with Neymar!
Credit: @k.mbappe

KEVIN DE BRUYNE

Watch out City fans – is De Bruyne planning a move to Paris?
Credit: @kevindebruyne

PIERRE-EMERICK AUBAMEYANG

A comic creation gives the Barcelona striker a big Spider-man vibe!
Credit: @auba

SADIO MANE

Mane has so many trophies, he has to keep some in his bed!
Credit: @sadiomaneofficiel

AARON RAMSDALE

Arsenal fans loved seeing the ace goalkeeper in this classic kit!
Credit: @aaronramsdale

HARRY KANE

The England hero hangs out with the boys on a private jet!
Credit: @harrykane

EUROPE'S TOP TEENS!

All aged under 20, this group of awesome youngsters will be huge stars in the European game very soon – some of them are so good they already are!

JUDE BELLINGHAM

Age: 19 ⚽ Central midfield
Borussia Dortmund ⚽ England

England are lucky to have the best teenage central midfielder right now. Bellingham began his career with Birmingham, before a switch to Dortmund in Germany saw him really show off his world-class talent. An England regular, this all-action star has the skills, power and footy brain to boss any match.

GAVI

Age: 18 ⚽ Central midfield
Barcelona ⚽ Spain

Pablo Martin Paez Gavira – better known as Gavi – is one of the hottest teenagers in the world. An energetic, fearless central midfielder with a huge career ahead of him, he's already starring at Barcelona and also appeared for Spain at just 17. In a few years Gavi could be totally ruling La Liga and the Champions League.

JAMAL MUSIALA

Age: 19 ⚽ Midfield
Bayern Munich ⚽ Germany

Musiala doesn't turn 20 until February 2023 and has years ahead of him to earn his place as a Bayern Munich and Germany great. His skills mean he can play as an attacking midfielder but also work hard to stop opposition attacks. Musiala already has Bundesliga, FIFA Club World Cup, UEFA Super Cup and domestic cup trophies in his locker!

MALO GUSTO

Age: 19 ⚽ Right-back
Lyon ⚽ France

Having powerful, fast, athletic and intelligent full-backs is vital for any successful European team. That's exactly what young right-back Malo Gusto offers with his surging runs and solid tackling. In France he won praise for how he played against PSG's Neymar and last season was his breakthrough campaign.

FLORIAN WIRTZ

Age: 19 ⚽ Attacking midfield
Bayer Leverkusen ⚽ Germany

The goalscoring and goal creating teenager is smashing records and impressing hugely in Germany. Last season he became the youngest, at 18 years seven months and 12 days, to play 50 Bundesliga games having already reached ten league goals at a younger age than any other player. He also won his first Germany cap last season.

30 CHAMPIONS

2 Cristiano Ronaldo bagged 100 goals before any other player.

1 French club Marseille won the first Champions League.

3 Real Madrid won it three years in a row (2016, 2017, 2018).

4 Real Madrid hero Zinedine Zidane is the only coach to win it three times in a row.

5 Barcelona's Ansu Fati became the youngest scorer, aged 17 years 40 days in 2019.

6 Roma's Francesco Totti is the oldest scorer at 38 years 59 days.

7 Juventus have lost a record five Champions League finals.

9 No fans attended the 2020 final because of the pandemic.

8 A record crowd of 115,500 watched Barcelona v PSG in 1995.

10 Welshman Gareth Bale lifted the 2017 trophy with Real Madrid in Cardiff.

11 Bayern Munich lost the 2012 final in their own stadium.

12 Two clubs have won the final in their country – Juventus in 1996 and Dortmund in 1997.

13 Bayern striker Roy Makaay netted after just 10.12 seconds in 2007.

14 Goalkeeper Hans Jorg-Butt scored three Champions League goals.

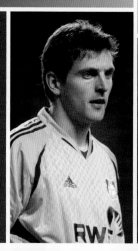

15 Lionel Messi scored five goals in one game for Barcelona.

56

LEAGUE FACTS

The 2022-23 season marks 30 years since the Champions League started in 1992, so check out these 30 facts...

16 Zlatan Ibrahimovic played for seven different Champions League clubs.

17 The only club Zlatan didn't score for in the competition was Manchester United.

18 Clarence Seedorf won four medals with three clubs – AC Milan (twice), Real Madrid and Ajax.

19 The Women's Champions League started in 2009. Before that it was the UEFA Women's Cup.

21 Liverpool, Manchester United, Chelsea, Manchester City, Arsenal, Tottenham, Newcastle, Leicester, Blackburn and Leeds are the English clubs to play in the full competition.

20 Group stage teams also enter their youth team into the UEFA Youth League.

22 Everton could have played in 2005-06 but they lost in qualifying against Villarreal.

23 Five English clubs – Liverpool, Manchester City, Manchester United, Tottenham and Chelsea – played in the 2017-18 season.

24 As well as four trophies, Sergio Ramos also got four red cards playing for Real Madrid.

25 DJ Marshmello performed the famous Champions League anthem on the pitch before the 2021 final.

26 Liverpool's Salah, Mane and Firmino each scored ten goals in 2017-18.

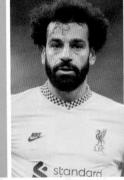

27 Before 2010, the final was always played on a Wednesday.

28 A club that wins the Champions League can earn around £60 million in prize money.

29 Erling Haaland scored 20 goals in his first 14 games and all before his 21st birthday.

30 The Champions League is 30 years old but the Premier League is too. That also started in 1992-93!

PITCH PERFECT?

Things are not always as they seem on a Premier League pitch. Ten changes have been made to the bottom picture – can you see them all?

1   2   3   4   5   6   7   8   9   10

ANSWERS ON PAGES 76-77

RAMSDALE

NAME: Aaron Ramsdale
CLUB: Arsenal
COUNTRY: England
POSITION: Goalkeeper
BORN: 14 May 1998
PREVIOUS CLUBS: Sheffield United, Bournemouth, Wimbledon (loan), Chesterfield (loan)

DID YOU KNOW?

Ramsdale's England debut in 2021 was a 10-0 win over San Marino. He was the first Arsenal goalkeeper to play for England since 2002.

KLOPP'S CODE CRACKERS

Liverpool boss Jurgen Klopp wants to keep his team selection a secret, so he's used a clever system. With the code below, work out the 11 players he has picked and write them down on the other page.

A B C D E F G

H I J K L M N

O P Q R S T U

V W X Y Z

IF PLAYERS WERE GAMING

Check out what would happen if these epic ballers used their slick footy skills to become computer characters...

KYLIAN MBAPPE
SONIC

Credit: Sega

Sonic is a super speedy hero who's always blitzing and gliding between anything in his path. That sounds just like the legendary France forward Mbappe!

JORDAN HENDERSON
MINECRAFT STEVE

Credit: Mojang

Henderson always digs in and battles hard for club and country, working his boots off to get a positive result. Steve from Minecraft shares those skills – just a shame he wears blue!

LUIS SUAREZ
SUPER MARIO

Matching the iconic Nintendo star, striker Luis Suarez has been on the scene for ages and always finds a way to beat the opposition... even if that means a sneaky move or two!

Credit: Nintendo

STARS

BERNARDO SILVA
JUST DANCE

Credit: Ubisoft

Have you seen the way Silva dances and grooves past players to set up his City team-mates? On a computer screen this guy would own the dance floor just like he owns a real-life pitch!

Credit: The LEGO Group Marvel

CAPTAIN AMERICA
CHRISTIAN PULISIC

KIM LITTLE
ZELDA

Credit: Nintendo

Arsenal and former Scotland ace Little has won awards and trophies all over the world. Both her and Zelda are full of magical powers that help them master their kingdoms!

Fans already call the USA international Captain America, so if Pulisic ever became a videogame character he'd have to be this one from the LEGO Marvel series!

SHOOT'S SUPER QUIZ

SECOND HALF

It's kick-off time for the second half of your SHOOT Super Quiz! Get your game face on and think hard about the answers to prove you're a clued-up fan!

1 Which successful women's international team is this?

usa

2 Is this part of a football ground known as the dugin, dugout or dugover?

dug-out

3 Is Southampton's James Ward-Prowse left or right footed?

Right foot

4 How many goals did Wayne Rooney net for England – 43, 53 or 63?

53

5 Is this impressive Portuguese forward Joao Felix, Andre Silva or Diogo Jota?

JOAO FELIX

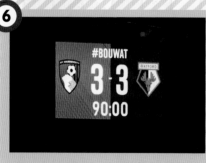

6 In cup competitions, how long is extra-time usually played for?

30 min

7 True or false? Goalkeepers are not allowed to score a goal.

true

8 Which other English team has Liverpool's Mo Salah played for?

Chelsea

9

Who is older – Gareth Southgate or Frank Lampard?

EOY

....

10

'Told Fordraf' is an anagram of which famous Premier League ground?

old Traffrok

....

11

What is the nickname of Brighton?

Dol or

....

12

Crystal Palace boss Patrick Vieira won three Premier League titles playing at which club?

Oisahal

....

13

Which English city is Aston Villa in?

....

14

Which national team does Real Madrid defender David Alaba play for?

....

15

In 2022 this defender was named England captain – who is it?

....

16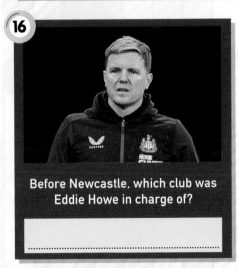

Before Newcastle, which club was Eddie Howe in charge of?

....

17

Which team plays at Elland Road?

....

18

ENGLAND v BRAZIL

WELCOME TO WEMBLEY

Which year did the new Wembley Stadium open – 1997, 2007 or 2017?

....

19

Which two Italian clubs share the iconic San Siro Stadium for home matches?

....

20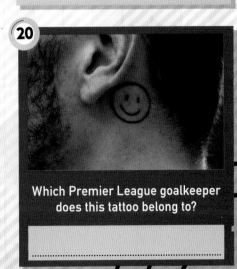

Which Premier League goalkeeper does this tattoo belong to?

....

ANSWERS ON PAGES 76-77

CAROLINE WEIR >

+ Caroline Weir has produced some massive displays and memorable goals in her career. The Scotland star tells SHOOT about scoring, joining Real Madrid and her future targets. +

You've enjoyed personal and team success. You must be pleased with your progress?

"I think my game has gone to new levels each season. That's what I work hard for and is always my ambition. It's great to be at a big club and obviously be with the national team as well. I have got quite a few caps and been to major tournaments. If you'd have told me as a five-year-old that this was what my career would look like I'd have been very happy. It has been a good couple of years."

What was moving to Real Madrid this summer like for you?

"From the moment I looked around the club, the facilities and the trophy room, so many European Cups, I knew I wanted to play here. It's one of the biggest clubs in the world, and growing up I used to have a Madrid shirt with Zidane on the back. He was my favourite player. It will be a new challenge for me, moving to Spain, playing in a new team and learning the language, but it's something I'm excited about and hopefully we can add to that big trophy cabinet."

Do you enjoy scoring memorable big-game goals?

"It's not something I go looking for. It's great that the coverage of the women's game is getting bigger. Obviously when they are good goals they get the right kind of attention. It is great to get recognition for the big goals and the more special goals are obviously nice."

Did your famous goals for City against Manchester United mean more?

"Maybe not for me personally, because I didn't look at the fixture and think that I've scored in three home derby games or whatever. The fans enjoyed it the most because it's a derby, they are always massive games with a good crowd. There was a lot of attention on those games and of course I loved scoring against United – it was really enjoyable and great to win, which was the most important thing."

Do you practice lobs and long-range shooting a lot?

"Definitely. Those goals are great when they come off in the big moment but it is about practice. It's a lot of repetition in training."

How cool is it to twice be nominated for FIFA's Puskas Award for best goal?

"Again that's not something you look at the season and aim for. You can't control those things, but I think in my first nomination there were four women and it's huge to be one of them. Then to be nominated again the next year, it just shows that people enjoyed the goal. It's cool to be included among some amazing players and amazing goals."

What would you say your role in the team is?

"It's like the number ten role attacking midfielder. I like picking the ball up in little pockets of space. It's about scoring and creating, keeping the ball as much as possible and trying to impact on games, whether that's assisting or scoring."

Do you switch off from football away from the pitch?

"I do have to forget about football because it gets a little bit too much. I think it's healthier and I work best when I have football and then just chill time. I have a little sausage dog and he keeps me entertained! I am quite sociable so I like to go out for dinner and things like that. I try not to watch too much football."

FACT FILE

CLUB: Real Madrid
COUNTRY: Scotland
POSITION: Attacking midfielder
BORN: 20 June 1995
PREVIOUS CLUBS: Manchester City, Liverpool, Bristol Academy, Arsenal, Hibernian

FOOTY FAVES...

FAVE PLAYER OF ALL TIME: *Zinedine Zidane*

FAVE SHIRT NUMBER: *10*

FAVE GROUND TO PLAY AT: *Parc des Princes, Paris*

FAVE GOAL SCORED: *First derby goal at the Etihad*

FAVE FOOTBALL MEMORY: *Qualifying and playing at the 2019 World Cup*

TRANSF£R CHALL£NG£

Here's a test of your transfer knowledge. Can you connect the player to the transfer amount they cost and the two clubs involved. It's a mega money match-up! To kick things off, we've done the first one for you. You're welcome!

PLAYER

FERRAN TORRES

RAPHAEL VARANE

GIANLUIGI DONNARUMMA

ALISSON

ROMELU LUKAKU

TRANSFER FEE

£34 million

£97.5 million

£46.7 million

FREE TRANSFER

£66.8 million

FROM

TO

FERNANDES

NAME: Bruno Fernandes
CLUB: Manchester United
COUNTRY: Portugal
POSITION: Attacking midfielder
BORN: 8 September 1994
PREVIOUS CLUBS: Sporting Lisbon, Sampdoria, Udinese, Novara

DID YOU KNOW?

In his first 117 games for The Red Devils, Fernandes scored an incredible 49 goals and made 39 assists. Wow!

Your WORLD CUP records

The World Cup is so special you should defo keep a record of all the big matches, moments and megastars. Qatar 2022, held between 21 November and 18 December, will be an awesome event so fill in the boxes below!

2022 WORLD CUP WINNERS

Argentina

2022 WORLD CUP RUNNERS-UP

France

TOP TRIO

The next men's World Cup in 2026 will be in the United States, Mexico and Canada with a record 48 nations involved.

GOLDEN BOOT (TOP SCORER) **TROPHY WINNER**

Mbappe

GOLDEN BALL (BEST PLAYER) **TROPHY WINNER**

Messi

BEST YOUNG PLAYER

BEST GOAL SCORED

BEST MANAGER

MY 2022 WORLD CUP FAVOURITE PLAYERS

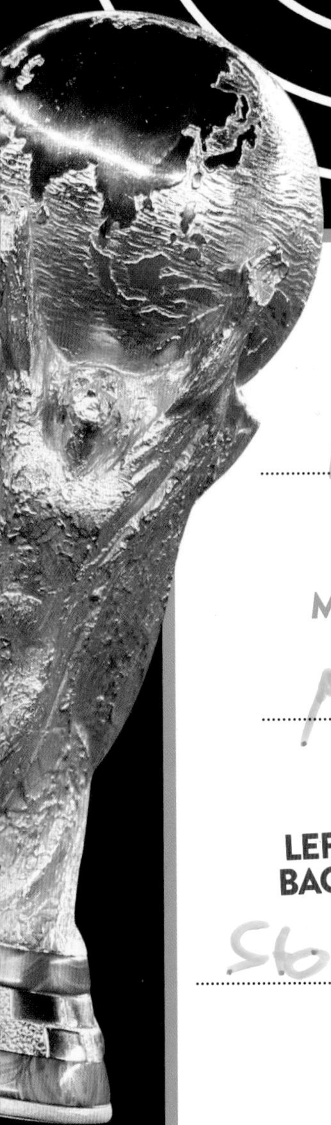

STRIKER
MeSSI

STRIKER
Kane

STRIKER
CR7

MIDFIELDER
Alvrez

MIDFIELDER
Foden

MIDFIELDER
camaIvinga

LEFT BACK
Stones

CENTRE BACK
walker

CENTRE BACK
Foffung

RIGHT BACK
Jaran

GOALKEEPER
EmI martenez

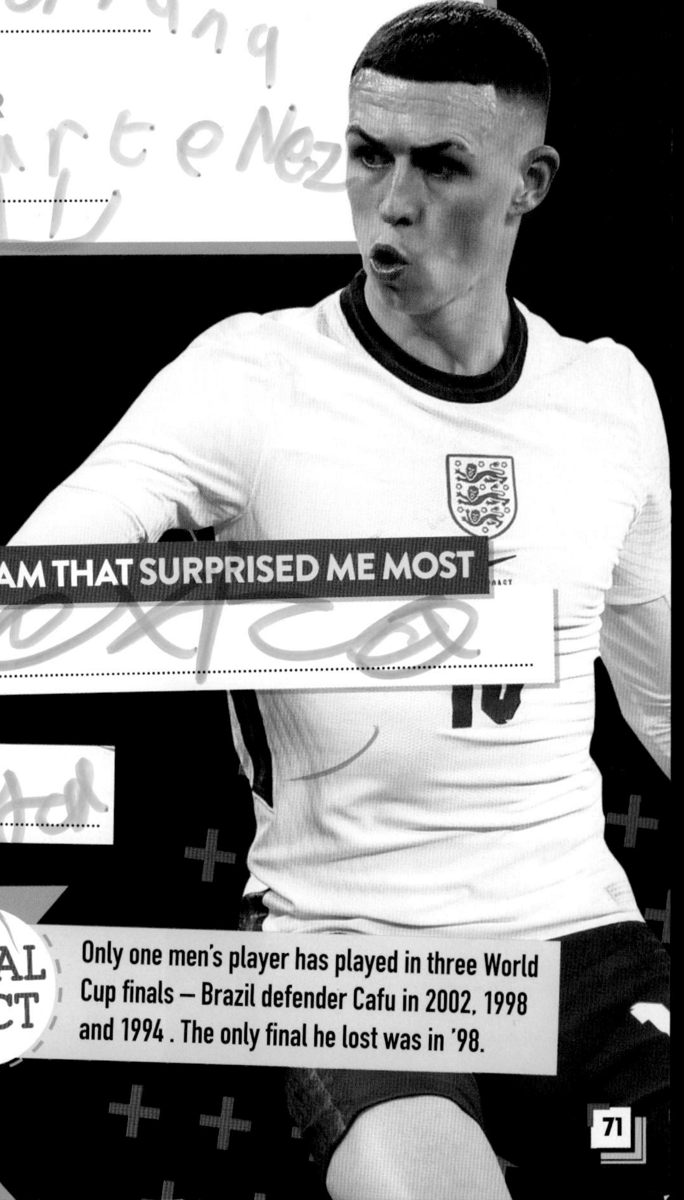

THE BEST WORLD CUP FANS
mexico

THE TEAM THAT SURPRISED ME MOST
mexico

MY FAVOURITE 2022 WORLD CUP MATCH
England V'S seneyal

GOAL KING
France striker Just Fontaine scored 13 goals at the 1958 World Cup. That's the highest total at a single competition!

FINAL FACT
Only one men's player has played in three World Cup finals – Brazil defender Cafu in 2002, 1998 and 1994 . The only final he lost was in '98.

2023

Good news – there's another World Cup to come in 2023! The Women's World Cup kicks off in July, so check out this quick guide to get you excited for another huge tournament.

TOP TEAMS

The planet's best nations will battle for the World Cup trophy starting on 20 July at New Zealand's Eden Park. That means the USA, Japan, Germany, France, Sweden, Spain, England, South Korea, Canada and 23 other top teams have their eyes on the prize. Over a billion fans watched coverage of the last World Cup in 2019 and in 2023 the audience and popularity will be even bigger!

THREE IN A ROW?

The mighty USA lifted the World Cup in 2019 and 2015. Can they now become the first country to win it three times in a row? Team USA is packed with goals, confidence and world-class players such as Alex Morgan, Lindsey Horan and Mallory Pugh. With young talent from midfielder Catarina Macario and forward Sophia Smith, they fancy their triple title chances!

AWESOME AUSSIES

The 2023 World Cup will be staged by Australia and New Zealand. Australia's big star is captain Sam Kerr – the dangerous Chelsea Women legend has scored more international goals than any other Aussie! With support by the likes of Caitlin Foord, Emily Gielnik, Hayley Raso and Kyah Simon – who have all appeared in the FA Women's Super League – the Matildas fear no-one!

WOMEN'S WORLD CUP

LETHAL LIONESSES

After hosting the Women's Euros in 2022 and loving the excitement and passion, England probably have their best chance of reaching their first World Cup final. In 2019 they made the semi-finals but now with more experience and superstars including Lucy Bronze, Ellen White, Fran Kirby, Nikita Parris and Beth Mead, Sarina Wiegman's squad is the best yet.

ENGLAND'S ENGLAND!
Forward Bethany England is also one of England's top goalscorers!

THINK BIG!

With 32 teams at this World Cup — which is eight more than in 2019 and 2014 — it will become the biggest women's competition. Watch out for double champions Germany aiming for their first final since 2007, Norway being powered by the returning Ada Hegerberg and Alexia Putellas and Jennifer Hermoso pulling the strings for Spain. *SHOOT* can't wait for the action!

MEGA MARTA
Brazil hero Marta scored a record 17th World Cup finals goal at the 2019 tournament.

2023 WOMEN'S WORLD CUP PREDICTIONS

WINNERS: England

GOLDEN BOOT: Ecoutoona

BEST PLAYER: Railling

2023

You've reached the end of your fun and fact-packed SHOOT Annual 2023... all that's left is to make your big guesses for next year and the rest of the season. Take your time and see if you can predict the future of football!

PREMIER LEAGUE 2023

WINNERS:

....

RUNNERS-UP:

....

GOLDEN BOOT:

....

PLAYER OF THE SEASON:

....

YOUNG PLAYER OF THE SEASON:

....

RELEGATED TEAMS:

....

....

....

....

CHAMPIONS LEAGUE 2023

WINNERS (MEN'S):

....

GOLDEN BOOT:

....

PLAYER OF THE SEASON:

....

WINNERS (WOMEN'S):

....

GOLDEN BOOT:

....

PLAYER OF THE SEASON:

....

CUP COMPETITIONS 2023

FA CUP WINNERS (MEN'S):

....

EFL CUP WINNERS:

....

FA CUP WINNERS (WOMEN'S):

....

LEAGUE CUP WINNERS:

FOOTY FUTURE+

WOMEN'S SUPER LEAGUE

WINNERS:

....

RUNNERS-UP:

....

GOLDEN BOOT:

....

PLAYER OF THE SEASON:

....

YOUNG PLAYER OF THE SEASON:

....

SUMMER ACTION

The UEFA Nations League semi-finals and final are between 14 to 18 June 2023, with the Women's World Cup starting a month later.

SCOTTISH PREMIERSHIP

WINNERS:

....

RUNNERS-UP:

....

GOLDEN BOOT:

....

PLAYER OF THE SEASON:

....

YOUNG PLAYER OF THE SEASON:

....

EUROPEAN LEAGUES

LA LIGA (SPAIN) WINNERS:

....

BUNDESLIGA (GERMANY) WINNERS:

....

LIGUE 1 (FRANCE) WINNERS:

....

SERIE A (ITALY) WINNERS:

....

TRANSFERS

BIGGEST TRANSFER:

....

SHOCK TRANSFER:

....

BIGGEST-SPENDING CLUB:

....

TEN-SE TIMES

Manchester United have a record 13 Premier League titles but 2023 will mark ten years since they last won the league.

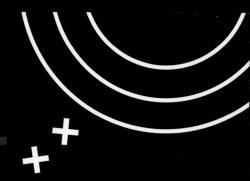

ANSWERS

10-11 SHOOT CUP RUN

1st Round: Captains armbands
A. Tyrone Mings
B. Kasper Schmeichel
C. Harry Kane

2nd Round: Spot the beard
A. Lionel Messi
B. Jurgen Klopp
C. Ilkay Gündogan

3rd Round: What's my number
A. 7   B.19   C. 66

QF: Badge Mash
A. Crystal Palace & Leicester City
B. Liverpool & Wolves
C. Tottenham & West Ham

SF: Country Connections
A. Conor Coady, England
B. Christian Pulisic, USA
C. Hugo Lloris, France

The Final: Mascot Match-up
A. Newcastle United
B. Manchester United
C. West Ham

Penalty Shoot-out:
52 seconds (Paolo Maldini in the 2005 final)

12 MYSTERY MANAGER

Manager 1: Steven Gerrard
Manager 2: Mikel Arteta
Manager 3: Pep Guardiola
Manager 4: Gareth Southgate

13 TRUE OR FALSE

1. False (he hasn't played in the Championship).
2. False (Old Trafford is, with approximately 73,000)
3. True
4. True
5. False (he hasn't won the Premier League)
6. True

16 SCRAMBLED STRIKERS

1. Timo Werner
2. Chris Wood
3. Michail Antonio
4. Jamie Vardy
5. Che Adams
6. Ivan Toney

22-23 WORLD CUP WORDSEARCH

26-27 SHOOT'S SUPER QUIZ - 1ST HALF

1. Brentford
2. Ruben Dias
3. Tottenham Stadium
4. Germany
5. Ralf Rangnick
6. Derby County
7. Zinedine Zidane
8. Right-back
9. Chelsea & Liverpool
10. Fulham
11. Dutch
12. False
13. Video Assistant Referee
14. Ten
15. Portugal

16. West Ham
17. Sam Kerr
18. Barcelona
19. True
20. 10

30 KIT SWITCH

James Tavernier B, D, A
Ollie Watkins A, C, B
Raul Jimenez C, B, D
Trent Alexander-Arnold D, A, C

34 GOAL GREATS...

Sergio Aguero – 184
Wayne Rooney – 208
Peter Crouch – 108
Thierry Henry – 175
Luis Suarez – 69
Jermain Defoe – 162
Frank Lampard – 177

35 ...ASSIST RATES

Eden Hazard – 54
David Silva – 93
Olivier Giroud – 28
Jermaine Jenas – 26
David Beckham – 80
Cesc Fabregas – 111
Steven Gerrard – 92

36-37 EYE KNOW YOU!

1. James Milner
2. Kyle Walker
3. Jadon Sancho
4. Reece James
5. Karim Benzema
6. Bukayo Saka
7. Jonjo Shelvey
8. Jordan Pickford
9. Kalvin Phillips
10. Pierre-Emerick Aubameyang
11. Michail Antonio
12. Robert Lewandowski